SIGNATURES

Joseph Stroud

BOA EDITIONS LTD.:
AMERICAN POETS CONTINUUM SERIES

SIGNATURES

Joseph Stroud

BOA EDITIONS, LTD. • BROCKPORT NEW YORK • 1982

Grateful acknowledgement is made to the editors of the following publications in which some of these poems or earlier versions of them originally appeared: *Blackwell's Press, Bottomfish, Choice, Dryad, Ironwood, Quarry West.*

The epigrams to the three Han-shan poems and the title "As for Me, I Delight in the Everyday Way" are from Burton Watson's translations of Han-shan in his book, *Cold Mountain* (Columbia University Press). The Rolf Jacobsen epigram is from *Rolf Jacobsen: Twenty Poems* (Seventies Press) translated by Robert Bly. The Kenneth Rexroth epigram is from *The Collected Longer Poems of Kenneth Rexroth* (New Directions).

Designed and printed at the Visual Studies Workshop, Rochester, N.Y. Typeset by Open Studio, Rhinebeck, N.Y.

Publication of this book was made possible with the assistance of a grant from the Literature Program of the New York State Council on the Arts.

Cover photograph by Marilyn Anderson.

ISBN: 0-918526-38-8 Cloth
          0-918526-39-6 Paper

First Edition: October, 1982

BOA Editions, Ltd.
A. Poulin, Jr., Publisher
92 Park Avenue
Brockport, N.Y. 14420

*This book is dedicated with love
to my family: my father, Don Stroud,
my two brothers, Mike & Tim Stroud;
Ellen & Sam Scott, and Rachel Harris.*

CONTENTS

Part One: Proportions

Part Two: Solitudes

*Signatures of all things I am here to read, seaspawn
and seawrack, the nearing tide, that rusty boot.*
— Stephen Dedalus in ULYSSES

*The doctrine of Signatures —
The law by which we must make
Use of things is written in
The law by which they were made.
It is graven upon each
As its unique character.
The forms of being are the
Rules of life.*
— Kenneth Rexroth,
"The Dragon and the Unicorn"

PART ONE

PROPORTIONS

The lyf so short, the craft so long to lerne
— Chaucer

SIGNATURE

*Gentlemen! Prince Myshkin asserts that beauty
will save the world! But I assert that the reason
he has such playful ideas is that he is in love...
Tomorrow there will be no more time.*
— Ippolit in THE IDIOT

A dirt road through the Sangre de Cristo mountains,
Then down into Santo Domingo. Thunderheads
And the brief, skeletal lightning.
After Acoma.
After the grief of mudhuts and drunkeness,
The dirty bars in Flagstaff,
And the vista where the canyon ends and the void
Begins. To this.
One moment as in marble.
Forever clear.
The wet pines, the smell of thunder,
Santo Domingo shining ahead in the sudden sun,
And my love beside me.
That this Signature should last.
That I could hold this landscape, an island,
In me. By craft
Cohere the wreckage of love.
But the language fails. Always
The heart breaks into prose, fragments
Of Ippolit on the sun-lit balcony,
Everyone laughing as he talked on into the night,
The moon rising with Myshkin's impossible
Love,
The cold, continual stone of departure.

DRAGON

All day the sun builds its temple
                           though we perish
In that shining. Rilke in the rose garden
Discerned his paradise in the quiet vault of blooms
As the thorn brightened his blood
And the architecture of light began its walls
Around his brief and singing house.
                       Even the great beast elephant
Follows the lava flow where the earth gives up
Its sweetest grass. And at the *masuku*,
Tangled with growth, the odorless gas seeping
From fissures, he eats and breathes until the tower
Legs fold, and the whole hulk
                         topples down.
Vultures, jackals, the aardwolves who come to feed
On the carcass, stagger and collapse
In the corrupting air.
                  So the earth leaks
Its poison. And the silent, alien sun
Gives no sign to those voices
Down there, looking up, crying and reaching
As they go under.

BELOW MOUNT T'UI K'OY,
HOME OF THE GODS,
TODOS SANTOS CUCHUMATÁN,
GUATEMALAN HIGHLANDS

He stumbled all morning through the market,
Drunk and weeping, a young Mayan whose wife
Had died. Whenever he encountered someone he knew,
He'd stop and wail, waving his arms, and try
To embrace them. Most pushed him away,
Or ignored him. So he'd stand there like a child,
Forlorn, his face contorted with grief,
Lost among the piles of corn and peppers,
The baskets of bananas, avocados, and oranges,
The turkeys strung upside down, the careful
Pyramids of chicken eggs, the women
In their straw hats and rainbow *huipils*,
The men smoking cornsilk cigarettes,
Meat hanging from the butchers' stalls
(chorizo, goat heads, tripe, black livers),
As everyone talked, laughed, or bartered,
And young boys played soccer in the courtyard,
The Roman priest, like a thin raven, elbowing
His way through the crowds, rain clouds
Swarming from far down the coast, the sun
Shattered among the pines on the high ranges,
And weaving through all of it the sound
Of women who sang over a corpse in an earthen house,
Keening a music like distant surf breaking
Within the very heart of the mountain.

LABYRINTH

Night-mares. Hrothgar can't sleep.
The mead-hall is burning
And burning down the Shaper's fine words.
The gold and shields, the bronze swords
Plume in the flames. Grendel
Again has come. The night-walker, breaker
Of bone-locks, man-eater, beast
Of the Mere, Cain's blood. What sacrifice
Now, Ring-Danes? Our smoke rises
Into night, it drifts across the Archer
And the Sisters. It rings a nimbus
Around the moon. And no words come.
The *wyrd* works our life to dust
And smoke. And the lovers in the labyrinth
Follow the thread to their heart,
Its empty, burning halls,
Its night.

SIGNATURE (II)

All morning he lay in the tight, dark room,
His head resting on a porcelain block
As the tattooed boy fixed the opium
And held the pipe over a flame.
                              Then out
Into the heavy Calcutta sun, the light pouring
Onto the courtyard where women in magenta saris
Washed clothes against a red mud wall.
And where the corpse of a man sprawled over a chair —
Just there — naked, spider-boned, stiff.
He stood a long time gazing at the bizarre,
Angular posture.
                    So that is paradise,
He thought, caught in the flood of light and heat.
A bright cloud swirling around a blazing tree.
The golden linkage of order. A precise,
Jeweled machine oiled with music. The cold,
Marble palace inlaid with lapis lazuli, agate,
Mother of pearl. And all of it shining. The bones
Gathering out of the earth, dancing
And burning before the tusked, goat-faced beast
Gorged on meat. He thought.
                              Until the landscape
Altered, and everything began to crack
And flake like a painting, the colors
Washing out, the Signature disappearing
Down the road with those Bengali men
Squabbling and laughing as they pushed
And pulled a cart full of dung.

DESERT

The sun ascending in Guanajuato,
                              a blazing stone
Over the desert. And the goats out there,
Their horns curving back into the brain, rooted
Like the heat.
                So you have to go down
Under the tombs, to the dry, cool air of catacombs
Where the bones are piled higher than your head.
Down the corridor the mummies gesticulate death,
Miming all our human postures. The woman
With shriveled breasts and leather skin, holds
In the claw of her hand the nearly perfect fetus
She must have died from, its goat-like face
Blank as the moon.
                    No prophet down here to drink
The dark-clouding blood and warn of homecoming,
Though you've mixed your heart with honey and milk.
Coming out of the dark, up into the flowers
Of evening, you know the vision of that day ahead
When all the years will brighten in you,
And the loud sun will give up its process
For the silence, the black fires, the long night
Of the last house.

JUNGLE

This jungle house on stilts overlooking
A Samoan valley, the papaya and mango trees,
Black pigs rooting among coconut husks, vines
Seething with passion flowers, skinks
Skittering among the damp, tangled roots.
All of it a continual gorging.
This jungle will eat a carcass in hours.
The mold, worms, flies, grubs, beetles, fungus
Cramp into everything. Even the hard bone rots.
You walk along the gorgeous, white beaches
In the melt of sun and sluggish heat, among
The pulp-smell of jungle rot, the musk-smell
Of breadfruit, your flesh opening and the sweat
Oozing stinging crystals of salt.
And in the room at night: mosquitos and blood-gnats,
The metallic-sheened blue-green beetles, the geckos
Stuck to the walls, their golden cat-like eyes,
Land crabs scuttling over the floors, bats
As big as foxes screaming outside, everything
Swarming and smothering. So much like the heart,
And the continual labor of ripping out its lush
Grieving vines and flowers, breaking open
The mush-centered fruit, paring down
To stone, the clear splendor, the cruel arctic
Of that other love.

for Phil Dow

DOCUMENTARY

Bring the camera closer in. Focus
On the burning *ghat*. They've finished
The ceremony around the body, and are torching
The wooden pyre. See how the tongues of flame
Rise from the limbs. Zero in on the head —
I want you to catch the skull when it bursts.
Pan down the torso, the spine in ashes, the hips
Crumbling. Then dolly back for the scenic shot —
The Ganges flowing past. But keep the tension
Sharp, you might catch the silhouette
Of a river dolphin. Filter the lens
To bring the blue out of the mud-silt.
Now zoom down to the middle of the river,
That small boat, the boatman dumping a child
Overboard. Get his flex of muscle
As he struggles with the stone tied to the corpse.
Then back to the panorama, the vista. The storm
Rushing in. The lightning flashing far off
Over the river palace. The silver drizzle
Of rain. The quiet glow on the water.

INTERLUDE

For antelope two invisible boundaries exist.
If you cross the first, they will flee.
If you chance upon the second, they will attack.
The question is how to approach without
Touching either,
                              to find the posture
Which translates the heart.

SIGNATURE (III)

Tsangyang Gyatso was twelve years old
When they claimed him the new Dalai Lama.
Too late, for he had learned to love this world.
I can see him in the great palace at Lhasa
Standing among the strict monks and the immense
Hanging tanka of Vajrasattva. Each day
He performed the service and tended the spirit.
But at night he would slip out of the chambers
And steal down to the little town of Sho.
There in that warm, yellow room the women
Would undress for his pleasure.
                         Broken
From the continual divorce within, he wrote
His tiny poems of love. And one day left Lhasa,
Disappeared, to wander the ice and cliffs,
A beggar for the rest of his life.
                         Each year
In his mountain kingdom a tower festival
Is performed: the delicate Buddha paradise
Carved from blocks of frozen butter. At dawn
Amid the chanting, the turning prayer wheels,
They are tossed into fire and all our butter dreams
Rush out in flames.
                  Tsangyang Gyatso,
Your laughter was like a mountain, your weeping
Was a dragon with wings. You knew more than any of us
That such is the Signature of all things.

THE ROOM ABOVE THE WHITE ROSE

This steaming night in Vientiane. A filthy room,
The Laotian girl gone, lice in the bedsheets,
The Mama-san downstairs counting the money
And the hours. Outside, gunboats cruise the Mekong.
The Pathet Lao and Royalist troops stroll the streets,
Forever divorced in their deadly politic.
                                        All night
I listen to Rachel's voice on the tape,
Remembering those first years when we held
And held each other through the mornings, the orchard
Blossoming around us, the strawberries ripe
And blazing in the field.
                                And I think of that other marriage:
The monkey-rope hooked from Ishmael to Queequeg
As he sloshed over the dead hulk of whale,
All around him the sea rioting with waves and sharks.
All night the tape goes on, Rachel's words deepening
With the hours, the batteries running down,
The sound going bestial, disembodied,
                                        fading
Into the laughter and cursing of the soldiers
And whores leaving the White Rose, and mixing
With the faint, otherworld song of monks
Chanting in the Dragon Temple at dawn.

DOGS

Lahore. Rain. The mud streets of Peshawar.
Those women without faces, hooded, blurring
In the storm.
                    So the journey continues.
Through Khyber Pass with its bandit tribes
And their heavy, handcrafted guns. And on
Over the Hindu Kush, the huge outcroppings
Of stone, the high plateau. A snow kingdom.
Everything white and blinding. The sun
So much gold. The blue mosque at Kabul
And the desert beyond.
                            Finally to the village
Outside Kandahar, where they bring the dogs
Tasseled with plumes, harnessed in hemp ropes.
The men sit in a large circle, a kind of calmness
Around the rush when the dogs are cut loose
And lunge for each other's throats.
                                    All the heart's
Landscape. The violence that persists there.
The male throne speckled with blood.
                                    In the distance
The city in dusk is burning. You can hear
The muzzein's far-off singing, calling
The believers to prayer, as the women sit alone,
Huddled in their mud houses, and the moon rises,
Just rises,
            above everything.

MADRAS:
WIND, WINGS, AND LIGHT

The window opened out
                    under the huge canopy
Of a banyan tree. Each morning
I looked into that green palace
With its emerald parrots, lizards, the shrieking crows.
The sun filled my room, its white walls
Gleaming like ice.
                    Then the wind
Would rise off the Bay of Bengal
And all the leaves began talking in tongues.
It was a blood music, the gradual turning
To earth, heart
                    wards, the black crows
Hunched like miniature monks, the tree
A blazing temple.
                    And suddenly it all died down.
Complete silence. The quiet sun going on.
The brief glimpse among the shattered
And splintered leaves
                    of the dead kings dragging
Their crowns, of the angel's huge jeweled wing,
And the far-off, paradise
                    dragon light.

TRIPTYCH

1.

What did Adam see, turning from Paradise
And all the singing beasts, as he walked
With Eve into that other world?
                    Perhaps a vision
Of Akbar's ghost city with its gardens and mosque.
Maybe he glimpsed, under the great walls of the palace,
Amid the yellow wheat with its seed-pearls of grain,
The harvester shading his eyes, his thin
Skull face grinning under the cowl
As he leaned against his blade.

2.

After weeks of slashing through jungle,
Bernal Diaz finally glimpsed paradise —
                           over a blue lake
Gleamed the island city of Tenochtitlán, chalk-white
In the sun, towering with pyramids, the elegant roads
Floating over the water.
                    Later, fleeing
For his life, he turned for one last look,
And saw his companions being dragged
Up the pyramid's high altar, the air full
Of conch music, quetzal feathers, as the priests
Ripped open the Spaniards' chests
                          and the still beating heart
Was drawn forth. His final glimpse was of the corpses
As they tumbled down the steep
Dragon-carved, stone steps.

3.

What corrupts the heart?
                        Raskolnikov calculated
Each step to the murder house. His childhood
Did not save him — the dream memory of Mikolka
Whipping the horse across its face, the iron bar
Crashing over and over upon the horse's back,
Young Raskolnikov weeping as he cradled
The head in his arms.
                        Or noble Othello.
Desdemona on her bed among the wedding silks,
The candle a blue flower in her chamber,
As the Moor nursed his beast with doubt
And rage, his only love everywhere within him
Failing.

SIGNATURE (IV)

When I arrived at the gate of the Topkapi Palace,
She was sitting on the steps, crying into her hands,
A young girl, 12 or 13 years, but it was hard to tell,
The sound she made was both childlike and old.
Someone had tied a bear to a maple tree
And it sat on its haunches, pawing the air
As if begging for food or money.
When I came out from the palace,
She was still there, though she had stopped crying.
I looked off towards Hagia Sophia
Where the bear was now performing for a crowd.
I could hear the ships pass by on the Bosporous.
They made a huge sound. Like an empire.
Inhuman crossed with human grief. What is taken
Away from what has been given.

PARADISE FIRES

In Klungkung two boys squat on the ground
And hold between them a rooster, its neck
Stretched taut, as one carefully slits the throat.
And they let it go, flopping and flying,
Its frantic song cut short
As the blood flows out in a quiet fire.
                                      That other kingdom
Where the black fires don't burn. Where the dead
Blaze within a wooden bull, and Rangda —
The moon-faced demon with curved, tusking teeth —
Gives way to the good beast Barong, guardian
Of the graveyard, as the *kris* dancers roll
Over in the dirt with knives pressed against
Their chests — unharmed, blessed.
                                         Far up Mt. Bratan
The women come down to bathe in the lake.
Their skin shines in the late sun, the water
Flows over their breasts, and all over Bali
The night makes its music, a faint gamelan
Through the rice fields. The giant sea-snake
Coils tighter around the sea temple of Tanah Lot,
And the slow moon burns in its own pale flame.

CITY

Of course the heart is nothing
But muscle and blood, a chambered organ
The size of your fist, prone to attack
And failure. We can't include it
In modern poems, having given up
That old cadence for this slaughtered prose.
Once the heart was like a city,
Medieval, the cobbled streets led down
To the slums near the river. At night
Thieves were about. There's a butcher shop
By the stable where in the morning you can hear
The high screams of pigs as they are holstered
From the ceiling and their throats slit.
It's snowing now and there is a crowd gathered
Around the gallows as the Bishop in his gold robe
Forgives a sinner in the name of a greater King
Than the one in the castle on the hill,
That feeble old man who sits among his tapestries
Alone and afraid. Far off you can hear the airs
Of a minstrel singing *timor mortis conturbat me.*
And there are rumours going around:
Of strange inventions — glass which magnifies
The face in the moon — of wondrous, far off lands,
Cities made of gold, treasures of silk and spices,
Talking beasts, the rare unicorn. But here
The peasants are hungry, revolt is in the air.
An old man in a cluttered, upper room of the city
Sits at his desk and turns in his hands
The puckered, toad-like remains of a human heart,
And begins to calculate through reason and observation
Alone, how everything in God's earth or heaven
Can be known.

SIBYL

All morning the beast labors up from the valley
As the loud, black bees crash from sage to crown.
Beetles hunt in the thick honeyvines, in the rotting
Pulp of grapes and figs. The animal
Continues to climb the steep, winding path.
From this distance you can discern something
Clinging to its back. A stone stands up
And scatters off, stops, and turns its black,
Lizard eye.
          Closer now, you can make out
A hooded figure riding a mule
As the hard *chin-chink*
              chin-chink of hooves
Breaks through the insect drone. Everything
Quiets down. Even the pollen spiders crouch
Deeper in the blooms. The sun honeys
The earth, the heat weighs down like a mountain
As the beast comes on
              bearing the rigid, black-shawled
Old woman,
       and they continue past into the high gorge,
The Voice shriveled and mute
Among the sheer, granite cliffs above Delphi.

for Mort Marcus

INTERLUDE:
TO AN AUDIENCE

But what good is it
If they walk back into their normal lives
Unchanged?
                                    —Antoine Carpeaux

I would like to write a poem
That would embody in you something
Alien. A crow, for instance,
Clutching the branch of a dead oak
In a dry riverbed five miles outside
Of Hollister. A sleek, sharp bird, eyeing
The heap of white bones that was once a cow.
I would have you in that tree all day,
With the sun in its long, slow arc
Turning the fields around you into flames
Of weeds, the seedpods cracking in the heat,
The chattering sparrows nervous
Under your gaze. I want you to observe
In the distance, that sluggish man
As he stumbles through milkweed and thistles.
He'll try to stalk near, and finally stop
A hundred feet away, wipe his brow
With a sleeve, and swing the rifle
To his shoulder. I want you to look
Into that barrel for a long time
Before winging from the limb, the quick
Sun-burst and shattering of branches,
                                    as you fly,
Cawing and cursing over the sprawling,
Logical suburbs.

FORM: THE HEART, THE WHEEL,
THE EMPTINESS AT THE CENTER

In Pokhara
             under the peak of Machupuchare
A procession coils through the dirt streets
Led by a man lugging on his shoulder
The severed head of a goat.
                              They proceed
Down to the lake, past the king's summer palace,
And on to the island temple, chanting
And singing in their lilting tongue
How the glory in this bright blood, this dome
Of flesh, passes into dust
And is picked up again in the great slow wheel
That moves in the heart
                        whirling out flowers and amber,
Blue-winged birds which descend and cluster
Around the blood-pools left by the hanging throat
Borne on the shoulder of that man, two-headed
From this distance,
                    and gone now,
The music faint, drifting out over the lake.

KARPATHOS

Now the night goes out across my heart.
I have prepared for this moment
Feeling the blood whorl in me like those stars.
Like Andromeda appearing these nights
Thousands of years after.
                              Today they built
The *epitáphios,* a coffin of roses and lilies,
And bore it through the village as bells
Rang across the valley for the God who died.
Rachel sleeps in our bright stone house
Above the Aegean. We have come this far,
To this place, making our own peace
Out of the milk and stone of love.
                              Who can say
What is enough, or what diminishes?
We enter the labyrinth,
                    this time uncoiling the thread
From our heart, as we descend toward the dragon
And that faint, underworld singing.

SIGNATURE (V)

Everyone was in the kitchen preparing dinner
When Ellen found her cat under the cabin deck.
It had been dead two weeks. I took a shovel
And crouched between the posts into the damp,
Musky piles of lumber and newspapers.
I tried to pull him out by his hind legs
From beneath a tangle of boards and chickenwire.
He wouldn't budge. Clearing the pile
I discovered he'd plugged his head into the end
Of a pipe. He must have died peering
Through five feet of tunnel toward the dim light
At the end. Like the chimney of hell,
I thought as I pried him loose. The fur
Was eaten from around his skull. He looked
Like a Bosch angel — the fluffy,
Bloated trunk, white-tipped delicate paws, rigid
Snarled face, teeth bared, milky eyes.
I lifted him out with the shovel and carried him
To the meadow. I had prepared myself for ugliness
And the sick-sweet smell, but was shocked
As the worms dribbled from his mouth.
By now the sun was going down. I buried him
With the light slanting through the madrone and pines.
When I returned to the cabin, a bluegrass tune
Played on the radio, four voice harmony,
Guitar, fiddle, dulcimer, the music
Weaving out through the trees as pollen
Drifted in the fading shafts of light.
I thought of the good earth, and the body's
Slow season. The simple death, and the hard
Death. The burials we are called to.
The roots below in darkness, the flowering
Above in light and air. Love —
Into your company I work my life.

PROPORTIONS

For years I've lived with Breughel's painting
The Harvesters' Meal. At first I noticed just
The obvious. The men and women in the foreground,
Sitting on wheat sheaves, eating their simple meal
Of cheese and gruel. The pensive, sad-eyed man
Slicing bread, the woman lifting a pitcher of water
To her mouth.
              Then I moved on to the wheat fields,
The straw colors. The man with his curved scythe
Slashing the long stalks. Another man lugging
Heavy water jugs in each hand. Three women,
With sheaves on their shoulders, walk on a path
That will lead past the thatch-roofed houses
Toward a grove of trees where the tower of a church
Juts into the sky.
            For a long time I watched the dog
Back in the foreground. A spaniel of sorts,
Sniffing the earth, its white tail rigid.
                     Slowly
I became attracted to the expressions on faces.
The exhaustion of work on a summer day. The openness
In the heavy-lidded eyes. I kept wanting to see
The face of the young woman with her back to me.
Deeper in the painting two people greet
And talk. A man and woman, I think.
Behind them are two locust trees suffused with light,

Branches and leaves intermingled.
                              That held my attention
For a year. I started to consider color,
How it blended from the greens of the forest
Into the gold and amber of the fields,
The blue sky mottled with dust.
I began to dwell on balance, harmony, the music
Of landscape and work, the burden of earth,
Excess, and pleasure. The long, difficult craft
Of living.
              Recently I've been following
The road in the right background, the way
It rounds a small hill and disappears
Into what I imagine is a valley. Always
The other landscape the heart dreams
And yearns for. A place where we could dwell,
And trust, and walk on through a world
Renewed and fresh as far as the mind
Can create.

PART TWO

SOLITUDES

All night by the rose, rose —
  All night by the rose I lay;
Dared I not the rose steal,
  And yet I bore the flower away.

  — Anonymous, 14th Century

SONG

That long ago morning at Ruth's farm
When I hid in the wisteria
And watched hummingbirds. I thought
The ruby or gold that gleamed on their throats
Was the honeyed blood of flowers.
They would stick their piercing beaks
Into a crown of petals until their heads
Disappeared. The flowers blurred into wings
And the breathing I heard
Was the thin, moving stems of wisteria.
That night, my face pressed against the window,
I looked out into the dark
Where the moon drowned in the willows
By the pond. My heart, bloodstone,
Turned. The long night, that farm,
Those jeweled birds, all these gone years.
The horses standing quiet and huge
In the moon-crossing blackness.

LETTER TO RACHEL,
SEATTLE, SUMMER 1973

The whole wall was luminous and hung with black photos.
I could see the perfect, elegant bones shining
And the skull grin under the flesh
As the doctor traced his finger along the thin line
Of fracture.
           I remembered how the motorcycle
Couldn't turn the corner, and the slow buckling
Of the wheel as I went over the handles.
On the way to the hospital I thought of you,
And as the doctor worked over my face —
The quick, painless puncture of the needle,
His detached hands threading and sewing
As he hummed and talked of how our body
Is simply water's
           most intricate
Catch, its most complex vehicle for traveling
Over the earth — I was thinking how fragile
The body is,
         how fine
Those quiet mornings to wake and listen
To your breathing, the other miracle that flesh
Could catch
         this love, however brief
Or broken.

THE DEATH SO LARGE, THE HEART
LIKE NIGHT

The great whales are leaving, going out
Across the heart's landscape. Death
By death our days go on
                    like ships through the straits
Of Sunda, keeling with the weight of leviathans,
The severed thunderheads slung from their sides.
I think of Ishmael being towed in his small boat
Through the storming, dying circle of whales
To the quiet center: the bridal chamber of cows
With their trusting, playful young.
                              Here
It is evening on the coast at Parangtritis.
The sun goes out over the Java Sea as the huge
Vault of darkness comes on, shattered
With slow, wheeling stars.
                          And suddenly it's like being inside
The enormous throne of a whale's heart,
                           womb-dark,
The black blood glinting with light.

THE SINGING, THE DARKNESS, THE EARTH AS LANGUAGE

But how to accomodate death?
Tsang-kie invented writing, it is said,
By observing bird tracks around the lake.
From their prints he could tell what songs
Had been there. But the night birds
Leave no tracks. The owl under the sickle moon
Glides quietly through the dark,
Touches down only to seize its prey.
We know its home by the droppings
Of skulls
And bits of powdered bone.

GEODE

When Zarraga visited Bonnard's room
He found the painter surrounded by light,
The sun flashing off the white canvases.
Over the months they would fill with nudes
And still-lifes: the light of Le Cannet accented,
Exaggerated with magenta, crimson, vermillion,
As he colored his paradise.
                              For years
I tried to see women and landscapes
Through his eyes — sought to glimpse auburn
Among the shade of cedars, hints of lilac
In the ferns, cobalt, the sheen of tourmaline
On her. Then I fell in love.
                              Now I look
Through a huge country of silence, tracing
The different, foreign colors of night,
Working on my own canvas of a Greek island
And stone house, the valley far below
With its stark church and fields,
Rachel out on the terrace, kneeling
Over the cold water, washing her hair
In the granite light.

ABOVE MACHU PICCHU,
129 BAKER STREET, SAN FRANCISCO

in memory of Bob Waters,
murdered on the Avenues

Fifteen years ago I awoke
In a San Francisco room and understood
For the first time that I — and everyone
I knew — was truly alone. I looked
At the wall, the ashes in the fireplace,
The iguana in its glass cage, the floor
Scattered with poems. I got up,
Walked into the kitchen, and gazed out
Over the backyards toward the Panhandle
As one by one in the old Victorian houses
The lights came on.
                I didn't understand my grief,
Nor could I foresee how the years would lead me
Here, to these stone peaks in the Andes, looking
Down on the ruins of the last Inca city,
The broken terraces and moon temple of Machu Picchu,
As the sun seethes over the jungle and snow fields.
Nor how I have come to see that love can be
A way of learning how, and what, to praise
As I do now
             that distant morning
In that long ago room.

CORONACH

The boat drifts along the shore.
Its old wood is polished clean
And smooth
Like my grandfather who all his life
Waited for age to bring him
To this moment. He stops
To touch what he knows
Of the earth growing for him
His last garden — the small bean plants
With their fresh, new leaves,
Squash blossoms, pale shoots of corn.
The boat drifts with no one
Aboard, dragging its anchor forth
And back through emptiness,
While all the sorrows
Look out from the shore
Waiting for the departure to begin.
My grandfather sings to himself
Digging open the earth, preparing
His bed, as he dreams of flowers
That bloom in the dark,
Of the boat with its small cargo of light
Drifting
Under the earth.

DOLOR

Often in the quiet, dark hours before dawn,
I lie awake thinking of those other voices.
Tichborne in his Tower, pacing the night,
Singing his one poem before the absolute,
Final day. Or Traherne's child-like voice,
Lost for two hundred years, praising
A Lord of the common earth. Of Clare –
Grieving his entire life over the loss
Of Mary Joyce – who walked 30 miles a day
With a sack of poems over his shoulder
Trying to interest anyone in his song.
And Keats coming out of the damp, London night,
Feverish, coughing into a white scarf.
His last days with Severn beneath
The Spanish Steps. *I know the color*
Of this blood brings the seasons down
On all of us.
                    And I am overcome by the sorrow
Of it all. But grief is a place to begin,
A kind of clarity. Milton, exhausted and blind,
Dictating to his churlish, petulant daughters,
Began the Paradise at fifty-six.
And Hawthorne, twelve years alone in his room,
Conjured dragons of the human heart,
Perfecting the craft that could hold them
Focused and brutal.
                    In this quiet dark
I like to think of Emily, singing to herself,
As from her room she looks out forever
Toward the carriage approaching
With its silent, jealous driver.

THE GOLD COUNTRY:
HOTEL LEGER, MOKULMNE HILL,
REVISITED

The sound of rain on the roof was too loud.
I knew someone was making love in the next room.
I remembered all those years walking with Rachel
Through the orchard, the pine forest near Uruapan,
The stones and wheat and white Greek chapels of Karpathos,
Walking, it seemed, as if there was some place to get to.
I could feel the city begin to break apart,
All the careful bridges, the pavilions and lanes,
That fine old hotel with its marble floors
And ebony stairs, the quiet rooms with their windows
Overlooking the river, the snowy egrets, a lifetime
In praise of something larger than my life,
Crumbling.
           I got up and washed my face, stood looking
In the mirror looking back into the room, the rain
Louder now, wondering when I would leave, how
I would go out the door into the other city,
Making my way, building this time within me
A simple bare room, no window, an empty book
Of white pages, and a bed for sleeping.

CONTRAPPOSTO

When I was young I thought beauty ruled everything.
I believed all the old legends
And in the women of Gauguin who walked like gods
Among the Marquesas. I thought the mountain lion
That flashed below me in the Tehachapis
Was truly the king of my heart.
I imagined the horses foaming in the waves
Were what people meant when they said *joy*.
And I felt poetry was a way into the world.
I taught myself how to dream
Standing eight hours a day in a factory
Polishing and counting aluminum pans.
But one night on Karpathos, another morning
In a battered DC-3 banking over the ruins
Of Tikal, or the evening in a Montreal hotel
Waiting all night for a woman who never came —
I discovered this world is more
Than anyone could ever dream.
                                    At my mother's funeral
I knelt in the pew with my father and brothers
Thinking death had brought us here
To this poor homage, this farewell
To what the heart in all its splendor
Must learn to give back.

LETTER TO RACHEL. TWO FRAGMENTS.
THE ORCHARD AND THE DRAGON.

Last week fifty apple trees were torn
From the orchard. They bulldozed them over,
                                        chained
Each trunk to a tractor, and ripped the whole hulk
Out. Then dragged them into a huge medusa
Snaked with branches and leaves, and set it
On fire.
            At night the holes glow with a luminous light.
Rachel,
            each morning I wake without you.
All the graves in the orchard are open.

Near Tuscon I found the perfect white skull
Of a steer, the horns curving down
Over the empty sockets
                            so that all its sight
Must have been tipped with sharp bone,
The empty space of desert pierced
By a living crown.
                    Like our own vision —
All our landscapes, the days and nights together,
Flawed or proportioned by love,
Tipped with the dragon's cruel,
                                exacting horns.

POEM TO HAN-SHAN

Tell me, how shall I explain?

All night wandering through Santa Cruz
From bar to bar. 2:00 a.m., cold and drunk,
I walk out into the orchard.
                    Han-shan, if I talk to you
Across the years, it's because I have no other
Among these stark, winter trees. Perhaps all I'm doing
Is listening to my own dead, the words that are tombs,
Small burials. I know that finally to all things love
Leaves. But I never thought I would come here,
To this emptiness.
                Tell me, what did you see
Year after year among the sheer mountain cliffs?
What were your thoughts that last morning,
Stirring tea over the fire, watching
The mists rise from the river as your own fire
Began to grow in you, and the light went out
Across Cold Mountain?
                Han-shan,
If only this brief night would go on. And on.
Just the two of us, our companionship against the cold
And the dark, against the morning and all
Our promises.

52

LETTER TO RACHEL. TURNINGS.

Late February. The days grow longer.
The winter rains finally came, the drought
Has ended, and California again is green.
After a season of sulking, fighting, and breeding,
The elephant seals have left Año Nuevo beach.
Grey whales sound past Davenport
On their way to Baja. At Lighthouse Point
The monarchs leave the eucalyptus groves
On their long odyssey over the Rockies
To Canada. Hummingbirds return, garnet
Throated, from the jungles of Mexico.
The late winter light over the Pacific
Turns from pearl, to opal, to brass.
The almonds and acacias have blossomed.
The great Dragon rises from the east,
Orion and the Pleiades go down in the west.
Early evenings Aldebaran shines.
Killdeer sweep down on the San Lorenzo River.
I've pruned the peach, pear, and nectarine,
Cut back the honeysuckle and roses.
Soon I'll be turning the earth for a garden.
I've stopped drinking wine these cold nights.
And I keep promising myself a change
All these turning years with your absence.

POEM TO HAN-SHAN (II)

What is born in time must die;
All will be changed to dust and ashes.

All this earth and the late winter light.
All these turnings. The leaves
Drop from the pear tree, a sudden wind,
And the roses spill their petals in the mud.
Everything goes underground. The music of this season
Moves toward silence and nocturnes, empty
Snail shells pooled with gleams of rain.
                                    Han-shan,
How do we get by? The marriages turn
Toward divorce, the cluttered heart is swept clean
By grief or loss. The many cleavings. The little rooms
We live in. Lustre. The light
Diminishing.
                    Often I think of you
Alone on Cold Mountain, casting away each day,
Building your life around silence.
Each day I fashion a dwelling, a home
Of words. Sometimes the language
Is of cliffs. Or clouds. A river
Far below. A few pine trees on the ridge,
Some willows around a field. By evening
I'm ready to build a fire, and invite you to sit
And warm your hands.
                  Living alone
Is like this. The invention of a language,
The talk running out between us as the night
Builds its darkness, and the true words, the honest ones,
Glow in the ashes.

LETTER TO RACHEL. NEGATIVE.
THE ART OF SEEING.

In Weston's 1939 photograph, your mother
Floats on her back in a key-hole shaped
Pool. For a long time it reminded me
Of Millais' *Ophelia*, drowned among the lilies
And waterweeds, a bouquet of flowers
Clutched in her hands, her dress billowing
Folds of grief the lost glimpse in sleep.
But Charis is nude — her long, slender body
Floats in a peace nothing could disturb.
Not even death. Which isn't the reason
I keep coming back to it. But to glimpse
How of art a moment might be suspended,
And how Weston must have loved her
To catch that pose. How I love
To look, catching in her grace
The likeness, the subtle, haunting trace
Of you.

POEM TO HAN-SHAN (III)

Living in the mountains, mind ill at ease,
All I do is grieve at the passing years.

Five years I've looked into this orchard
Hoping to measure my life, only to find it empty
Of me.
       If I could weave into my heart all the nights,
The gold oriole in shadows, the moon
Inside each apple, the delicate jade-flower garden,
The song in the shape of fruit,
                or stone,
Or rain. Dream.
       All dream. I weave nothing
These long days watching the leaves fall and the trees
Holding on. And holding on.
             Outside my window
Lilacs are closing, there are new blossoms
In the strawberry field, the splintery water-tower
Is full and heavy in the sun. And now a hummingbird streams
From stem to stem of the fuschia.
I don't move. Han-shan,
         finally I see
What has been given me.

LETTER TO RACHEL

Now while the dark quiets the water
Let me begin.
                    Seven years the sun rose,
The mornings opened to flowering light
And night burned as our own paradise
Within the house we made of love.
                              That it should end
Is not news. The flowing years are full
Of signatures, moments even stone
Cannot contain. You were to me a way
Of seeing.
            Night through amber.
Or the Greek sun that day on the island,
A hundred bells in the air as we crossed the ridge
And saw the goats grazing under the turning leaves
Of olive trees, each with a small bell tethered
At its throat.
                    It is a true blessing — that music,
Those islands, the light, and your presence
Which colors so much of my life.

AS FOR ME,
I DELIGHT IN THE EVERYDAY WAY

Han-Shan

Each day the earth turns, each day
The sea rises, all the days the seasons
Are, the small lemon in its own time,
A face turning from the window in an old house,
The song we can always
Almost hear.
           There's a poetry to this life
No one will be able to write.
The horses come down the mountain at dusk.
We've all seen this. But who gives thanks?
And what about the lemon. When was the last time
Anyone brought that sweetness
                    to their face?
Of each loss there is an opening.
To find a voice for love is a way
Of loving.
How all the deaths and griefs rush out of you
When you hold the little lemon in the cup
Of your hand. How easy it is to forget
These poor daily rags we wear
Shine brighter than the silks of kings.

SIMPLE GIFTS

Let the young rain of tears come.
Let the calm hands of grief come.
It's not all as evil as you think.
　　　　　　　—Rolf Jacobsen

There are the hard days, the long nights
Wandering around inside myself,
Desolate, confused,
When I sometimes think of Kirby's old walnut tree
With its roots tangled in the leach lines.
How it has struggled year
Through year — in drought, storms, and frost —
To bring forth its small crop of green fruit.
And how we pick them, shuck off the thick skins,
And place the nuts on a rack to dry
For those winter nights when we'll sit
Around the fire with friends, and talk
As we open the wine, slice the apples and cheese,
And crack the shells to eat the earthsweet,
Gnarled seeds.

for Kirby & Anita Wilkins and Nick & Sue Roberts

FESTIVAL

We are at the gate above the river.
Peach trees surround the pavilion.
It is the time of the Emperor's feast,
The bounty of his riches and exquisite ladies.
Over there is Li Po, drunk and sick
On rice wine. They unscroll the silk
Before him. The crowd is quiet. Error
Is not allowed. Li Po has to be held,
The brush shakes in his hand. Suddenly
The poem lurches out. A sword in sunlight.
Our broken machine of language at last
At flow with the river. Fireworks
And sparklers cast light on the water.
The lamps are lit on the fragile trees.
Do you see the Emperor, abandoned and alone,
In the crowd of weeping faces?

SOLSTICE

The gold wine of Kos. Late afternoon
Below the Asklepion
      dreaming of those Berkeley
Summer evenings, those quiet, clear years
I once had. The walks along the California coast
Near Albion. Dinners at the Hotel du Midi.
And the night I first entered the amber glass
Of *Les Enfants du Paradis*. What did I have then
That all these years since has left me
Richer and less afraid? As now
        on this island
In a small, Turkish village, I sit among olive
And fig trees, surrounded by stone white walls,
Everywhere the scent of lemons, and prepare
For the honeyed ruins of deep summer, for those bees
With their deadly, droning voices.

NAMING

Summer in the Tehachapi Mountains.
A broken waterwheel, its scoop-troughs
Splintered and empty. Rabbit brush.
Owl's clover. And Grandfather near the pond
Pointing out the names of things —
Cottonwood, manzanita, rose quartz, quail —
His voice full of tenderness.
It was the first time I ever knew sound
As a kind of recognition or praise.
                            Near the end
Of his life, a stroke took away his speech.
He would sit on the porch, mute, and watch
The sun wear down the day.
                            But I remember
The summers when we picked filaree
And stuffed them in our pockets
Where they coiled like clock springs.
We'd stroll back to the cabin at dusk.
Once we stayed late, watching dragonflies
Dip over the pond. It was dark
By the time we reached the porch.
We could hear the men talking inside
And smell the potatoes and onions frying
In the black skillet. He put his arm around
My shoulder, and we looked up into the deep
Catch of night, as slowly he began to name
The far off, alien stars.

for Sam Scott

AUTUMN. GRACE. THE SIGNATURES.

1.

Rain
And the first cold night
After a summer of sleeping between sheets.
Restless, I lie awake for hours
Brooding over the wreckage of years.
As the storm thunders in from the Pacific,
I get up and fumble for blankets in the dark.
They smell of cedar
After months of being cramped in a dresser.
I pile them on the bed
And lie back dreaming of those nights
From my childhood
When I imagined the rumpled blankets
To be a sea churned by storms
Where I sailed in my little boat
With the ocean of stars turning
Outside my window.
I smile at the child I was.
And I remember Issa's last bed,
The broken-roofed shed he died in,
The drift of snow filling that quiet night.
And I think of the last poem they found
Tucked under his pillow —
There are thanks to be given.
This snow on my blanket
It too falls from heaven.

2.

A deer came this morning to feed
On the last leaves of the peach tree.
A doe. She turned her face to me
And stopped. We stood there
Gazing across the distance —
Two creatures measuring the immense
Difference of blood and star drift.
Her brown, almost sad, sloe eyes,
The large, delicate ears
With their thin branching of veins.
The next moment, she was gone.
And when I looked again
She had stopped on the ridge,
Her head turned, peering
Back, before she flicked
And disappeared. Yes,
There must be a love
Worth waiting all my life
For.

3.

The garden's last ripe, swollen tomato.
I lay it on the cutting board
And with a fine-edged knife
Slice it clean through.
Both halves plop over —
And there is autumn's city
With its bloody seed-shine of waterways
And canals, amber bridges and tiny boats,
A labyrinth surrounding at the center
The ice palace of fresh snow and silence.

4.

Let the day begin with its light.
For once, let the mothers and fathers sleep late.
Let the chickens in the mud
Scratch their own inscrutable chicken poetry.
Let the clothes hang from the line
In the rain.
Allow the crickets under the woodpile
One more day of their small music.
Soon everything will be clean
And bare, a fine inner blazing as the leaves
Drop, and the air is tinged with oak
Burning across the fields.
Let the dry skeletons of cornstalks
Scrape in the wind
And the sunflowers droop heavy heads
Spilling their crown of seeds.
Let the pearls on the webs in the garden
Gleam a thousand suns
As the silent sun hazes its light
Around everything I must lose.
Let the night build its darkness,
And the earth close once more
And at last, become quiet.

5.

Hunter moon. Clarity.
A room fashioned inside me.
Bare and clean. White walls
And one window. The short days
And the greater night to prepare for.
A leanness. The simple joy
Of being still. Solitude.
The single tree with its fruit
And loveliness of leaves
Gone. What the heart
Remembers. Compassion.
What did Myshkin feel
Lying in that room with Rogozhin
Next to the body of the only woman
He ever loved?

6.

I take heart in the simple act
Of planting these iceland poppies.
It's a mystery to me
How they will find something in this freezing earth
To grow out of, and flower.
It's the light of autumn I love,
The opal sheen as it pools the ocean,
The old brass of the hills,
A gathering of all the years,
And the leaves beginning their final
Gold burning, letting go, going
Under. The freshness the rain leaves,
The windows everywhere clear
Without the reflection of things
In them. If I had my life to live again,
How could I choose more than this?
Down on my knees, scooping handfuls of earth,

I recall the valley outside Jalalabad
With its melon fields and orange groves,
Where I stopped a farmer in his wagon,
Bought a melon, broke it open on a stone,
And sat by the road eating the crisp,
Sun-glazed fruit under the snow peaks
Of the Hindu Kush. From that distant moment
To this. All the Signatures. All
The turnings. The grace that somehow
Allows us this voyage from joy
To joy.

for Tim Stroud

Joseph Stroud was born in Glendale, California, 1943, and
educated at the University of San Francisco, California State
University at Los Angeles, and San Francisco State University.
His first book, *IN THE SLEEP OF RIVERS*, was published by
Capra Press (Santa Barbara, 1974). He lives in Santa Cruz,
California, and teaches at Cabrillo College.

photograph: Dan Harper

Signatures has been issued in a first edition of twelve hundred copies, of which six hundred are in paper and five hundred and fifty are in cloth. An additional fifty copies have been specially bound by Gene Eckert in quarter-cloth and French papers over boards: ten copies, numbered I-X and signed, include a poem in holograph by Joseph Stroud; twenty-six copies, lettered A-Z, have been signed by Joseph Stroud; and fourteen copies, numbered i-xiv and signed by Joseph Stroud, have been retained by the publisher for presentation purposes.